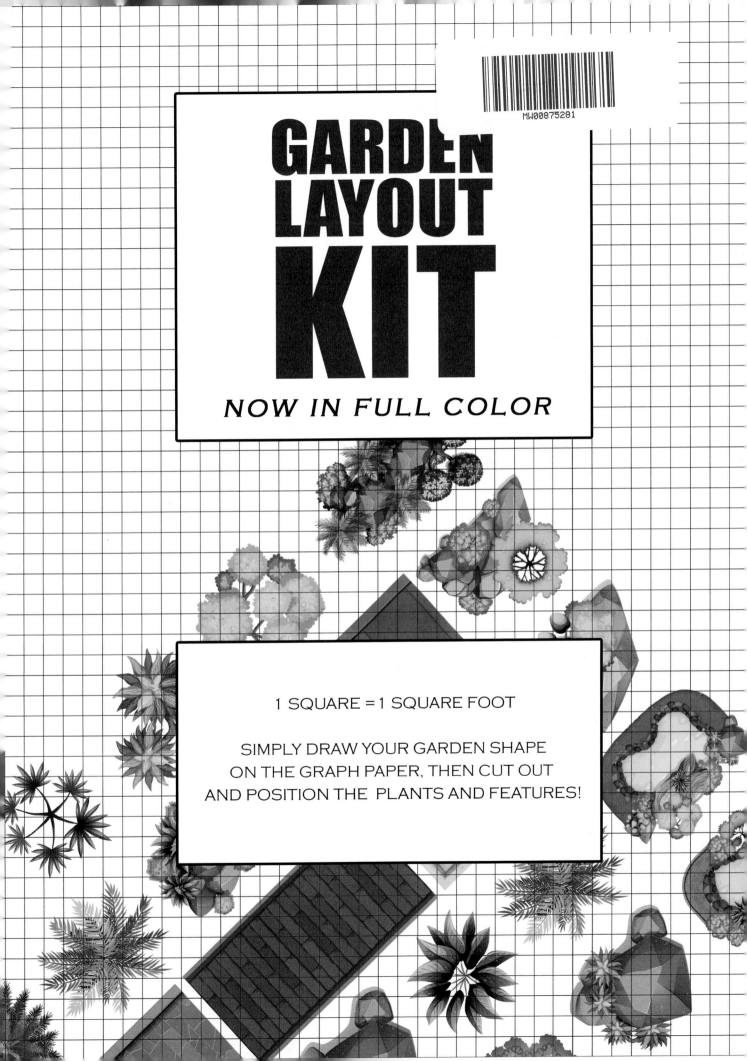

GARDEN LAYOUT KIT

NOW IN FULL COLOR

1 SQUARE = 1 SQUARE FOOT

SIMPLY DRAW YOUR GARDEN SHAPE
ON THE GRAPH PAPER, THEN CUT OUT
AND POSITION THE PLANTS AND FEATURES!

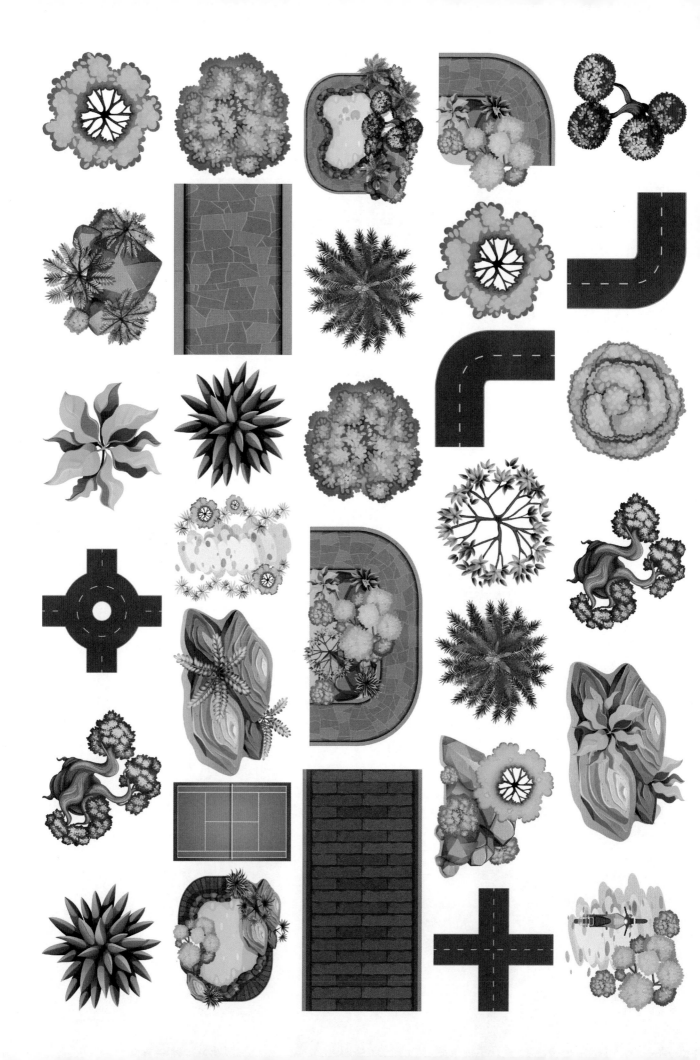

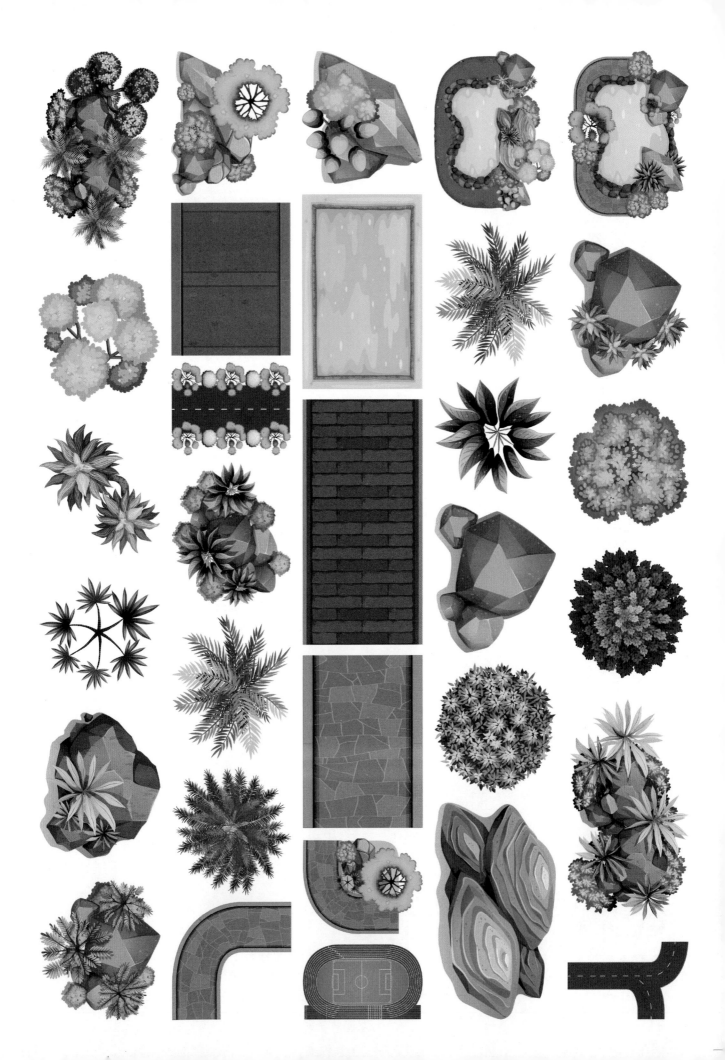

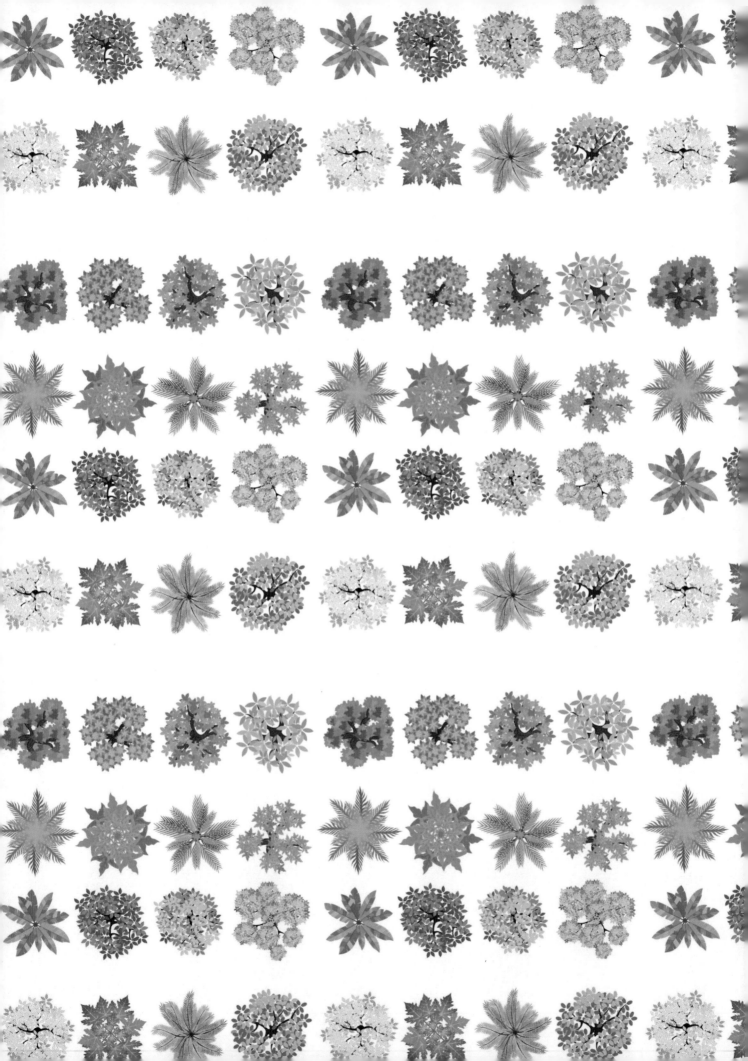

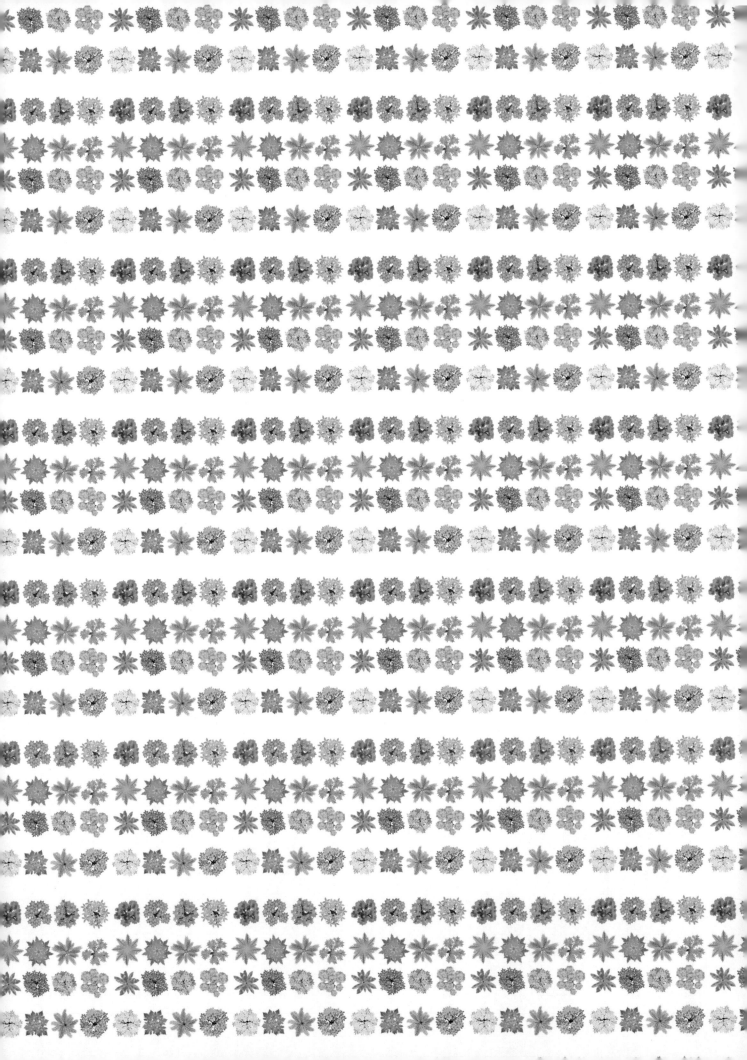

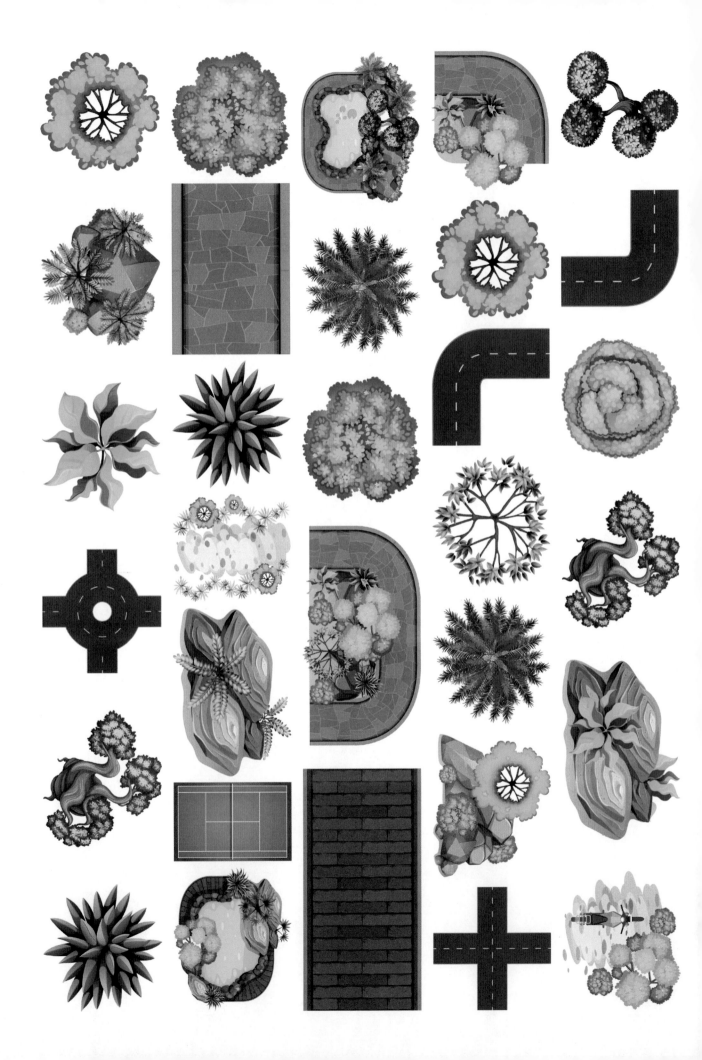

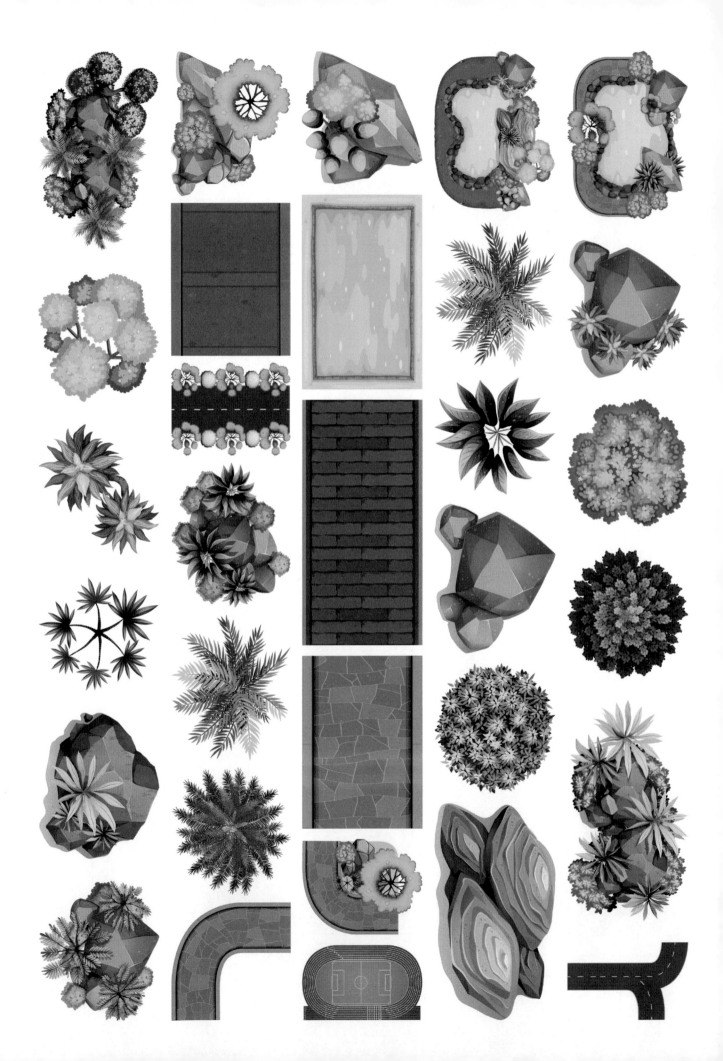

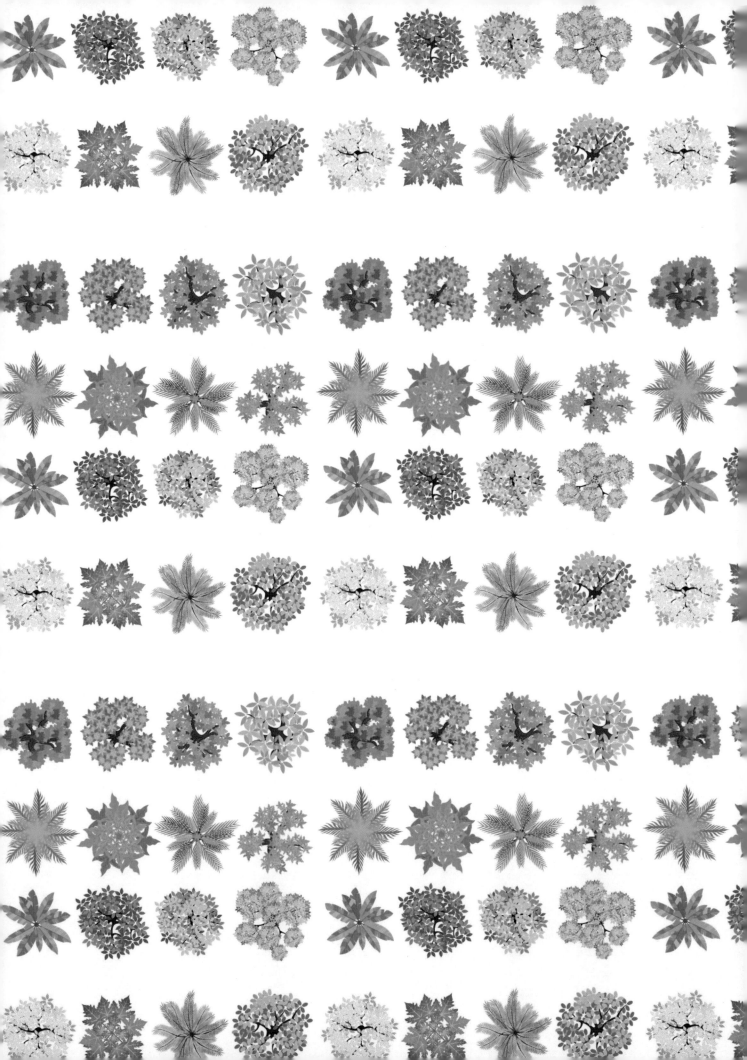

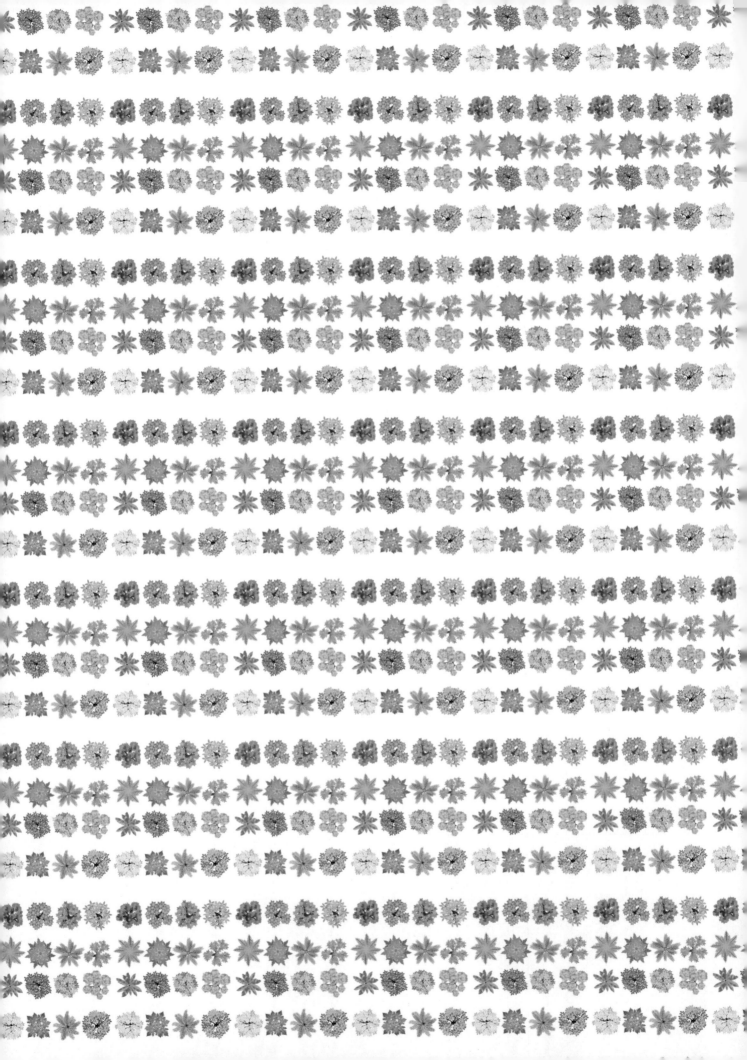

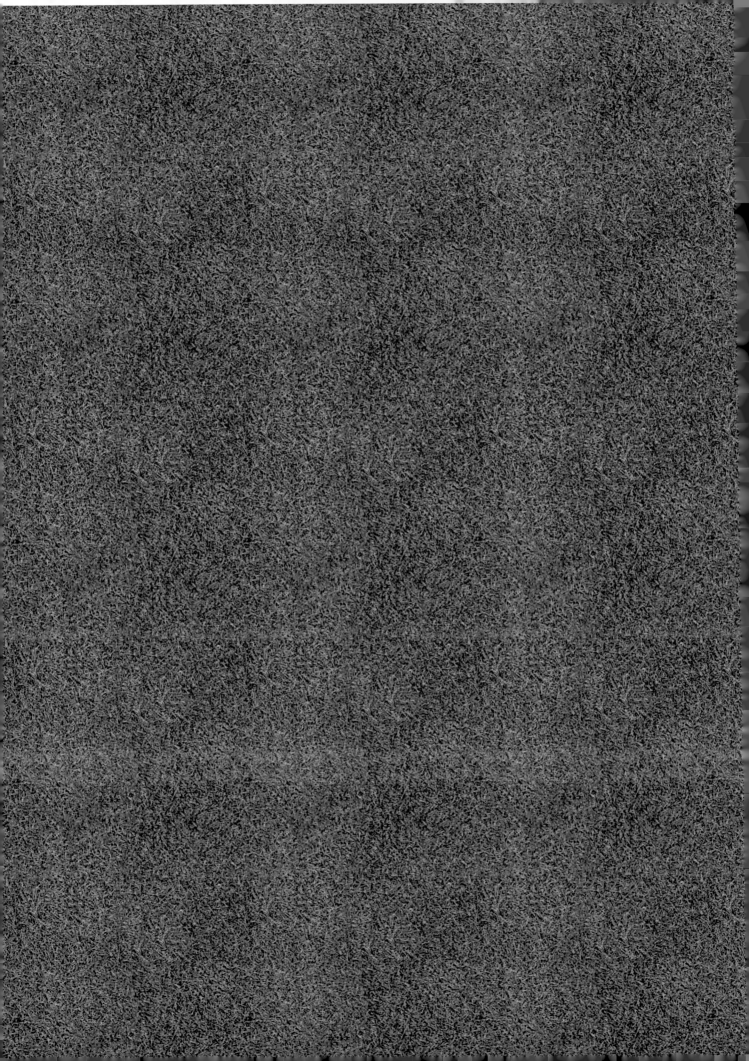

Made in the USA
Las Vegas, NV
01 February 2024

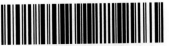